Parenting with Humor

Featuring Cartoons From
Air Mail
The New Yorker
The Wall Street Journal
and more!

Front Cover illustration: Roz Chast
Back Cover illustration: Will Santino
Introduction: Bob Mankoff
Editor: Darren Kornblut

Cartoon Collections, LLC
10 Grand Central, 29th Floor
New York, NY 10017

For cartoon licensing information visit www.cartoonstock.com
Create a personalized version of this book at www.cartoonstockgifts.com

First edition published 2024

Item # 47624
ISBN: 978-1-963079-15-9

Introduction

Ladies and Gentlemen, boys and girls, cartoon lovers and parents of all techniques, lend me your imaginations! Welcome to this wild ride of a book, where pen and ink meet diaper genies and ABC blocks. As the one-time editor of *The New Yorker*'s cartoon desk, I, Bob Mankoff, have had the pleasure of sifting through tens of thousands of cartoons, many of which drew hearty chuckles and even, dare I say, the occasional belly laugh.

Now, it's time for a unique adventure — a whirlwind tour of parenting through the lighthearted lens of cartoons. Why parenting, you ask? Well, for one, it's the world's oldest profession (with apologies to certain others). And two, there's no richer vein of humor than the trials and tribulations, the joys and jitteriness of raising a small human. You could say it's as ripe for satire as it is for self-doubt.

So, here we are, about to embark on this journey where cartoons become the parents and the parents, well, they become the punchline. We've got a collection of some of the best, most hilarious parenting cartoons, compiled not only to tickle your funny bone, but to remind you of the absurdity, the beauty, and the universality of the parenting experience.

This is not just a book of cartoons, it's an homage to every mom who's survived the "terrible twos," every dad who's played dress-up with his daughter, and every parent who's been bewildered, amused, and deeply moved by the odyssey that is raising a child. Enjoy!

"You can be whatever you want to be,
but you'll probably turn out like me."

"He looks just like you."

JON ADAMS

"My youngest is at the age when she can barely comprehend cost effective analysis."

"Me? I thought you were raising them."

"He's at that annoying age where they're always testing you."

"When I was your age, I was an adult."

"We won't know till they're older which one is the evil twin."

"I'm not his mom anymore—now I'm his life coach."

"She does this when she's tired."

"But you can't miss her second-grade
first-semester graduation!"

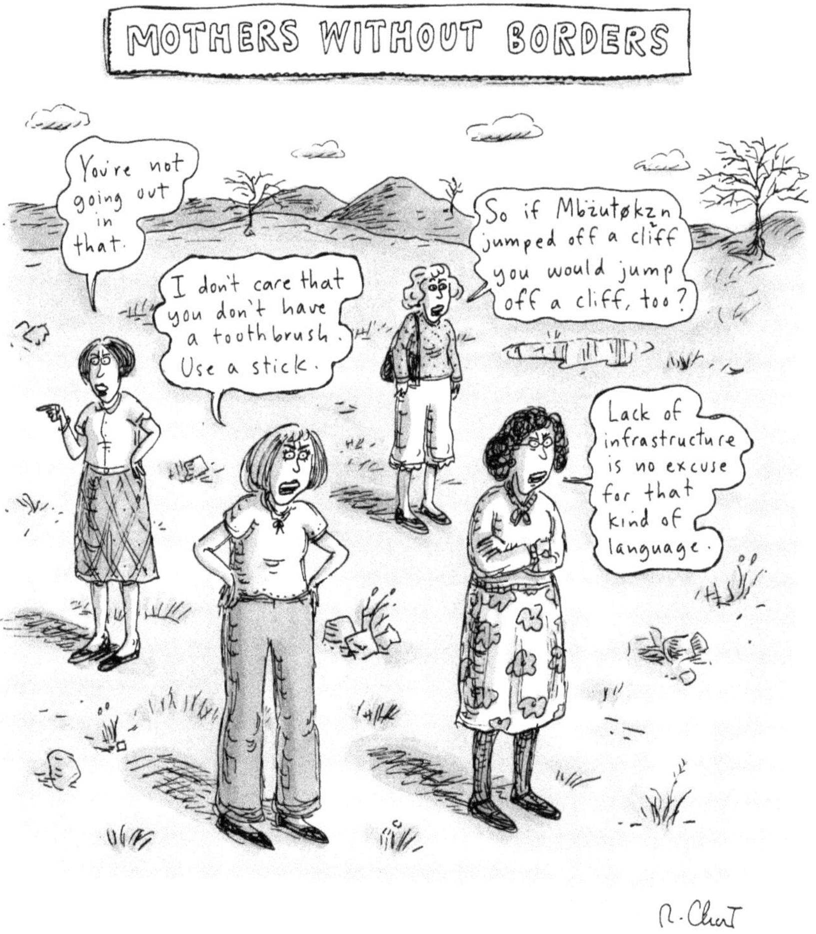
MOTHERS WITHOUT BORDERS
You're not going out in that.
I don't care that you don't have a toothbrush. Use a stick.
So if Mbz̈utøkzn jumped off a cliff you would jump off a cliff, too?
Lack of infrastructure is no excuse for that kind of language.
R. Chast

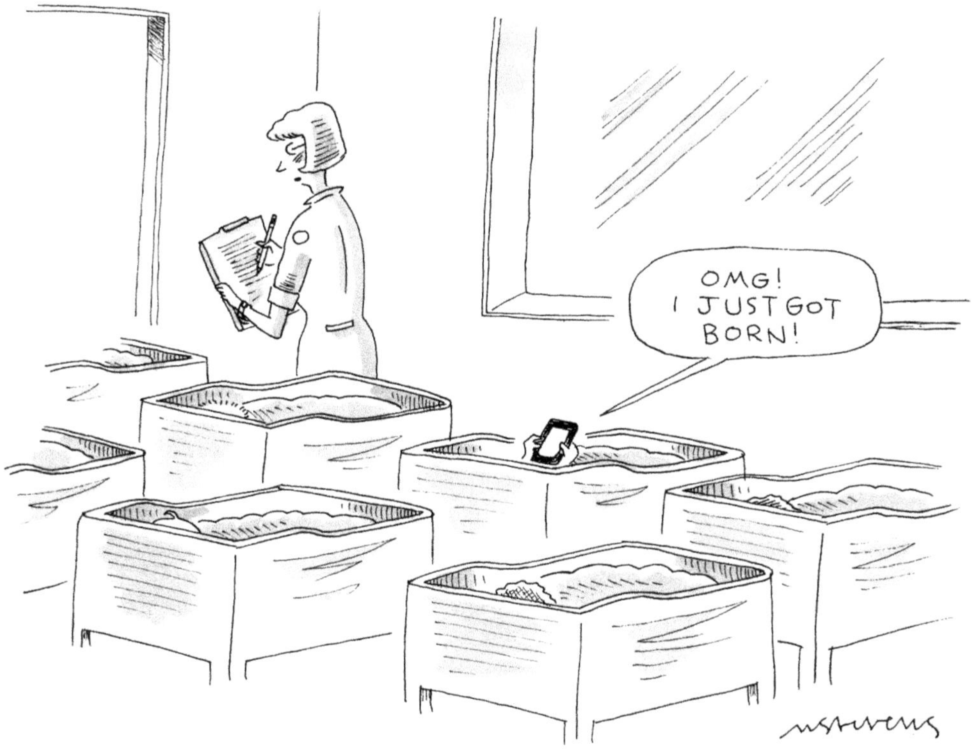
OMG! I JUST GOT BORN!
mstevens

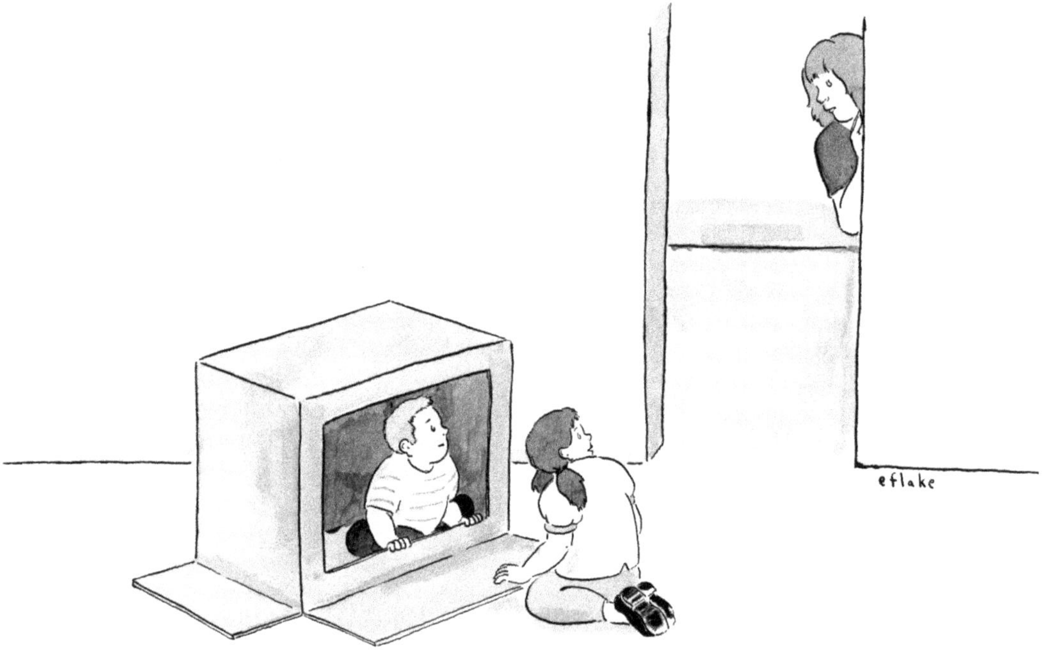
eflake

"We're playing YouTube."

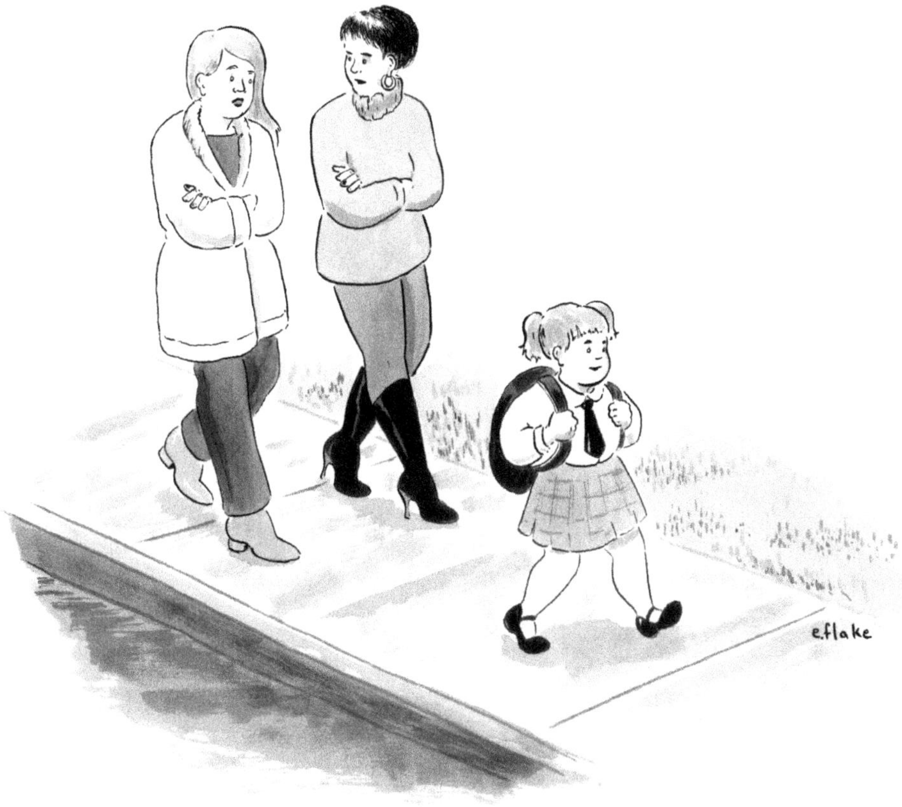
e.flake

"It wasn't our first choice of schools, but we had a Groupon for it, so what the hell."

"I'm Jewish and Don is Catholic, but we're raising the kids as wolves."

"O.K., Mom, I'm off the plane. I'll call you when I check into the hotel, and when I check out of the hotel, when I get on the plane home, and when I get off the plane home, and I'll call you when I'm in the driveway—glad you're not worrying."

"I just worry that we won't be able to provide the same level of crap that our parents gave us."

"Try and tell me what's bothering you—use your S.A.T. words."

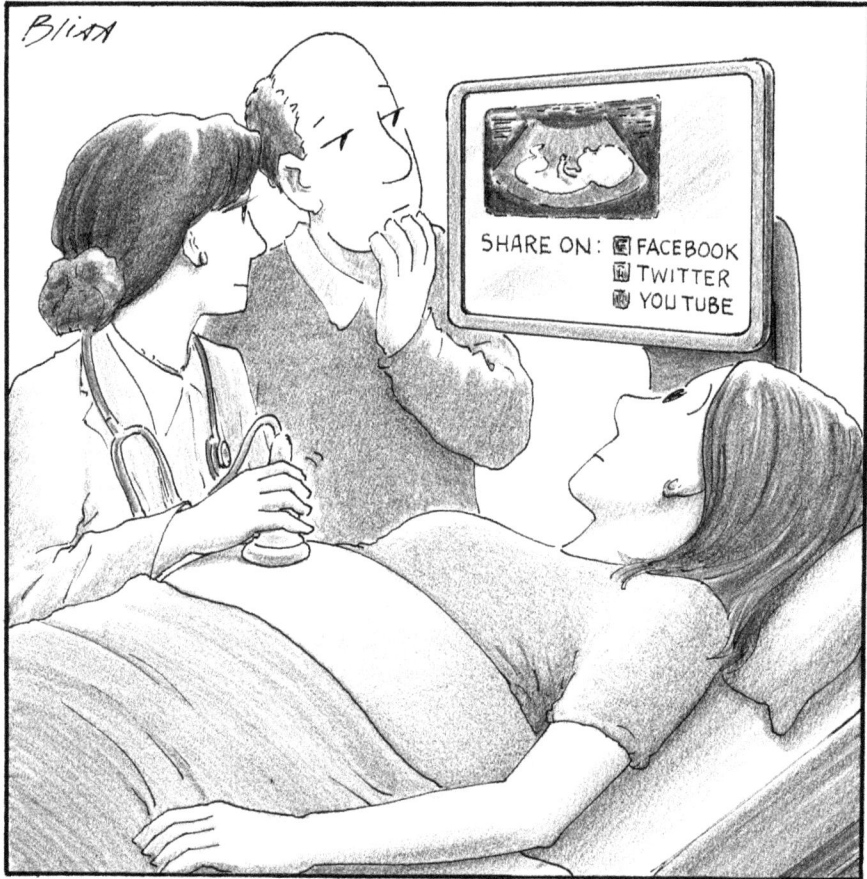

SHARE ON: ☐ FACEBOOK
☐ TWITTER
☐ YOU TUBE

"It gets easier the second time."

"I vary her diet with a wide variety of pasta shapes."

"I can't protect you from everything, but I can read you stories that make you believe I can protect you from everything."

"My wife is recording everything the kids do until they leave for college. Then I'll binge-watch them grow up."

"Sometimes I feel the only thing keeping us together is our fear of the children."

"Mommy! Daddy! Wake up! You only have thirty or forty years left to live!"

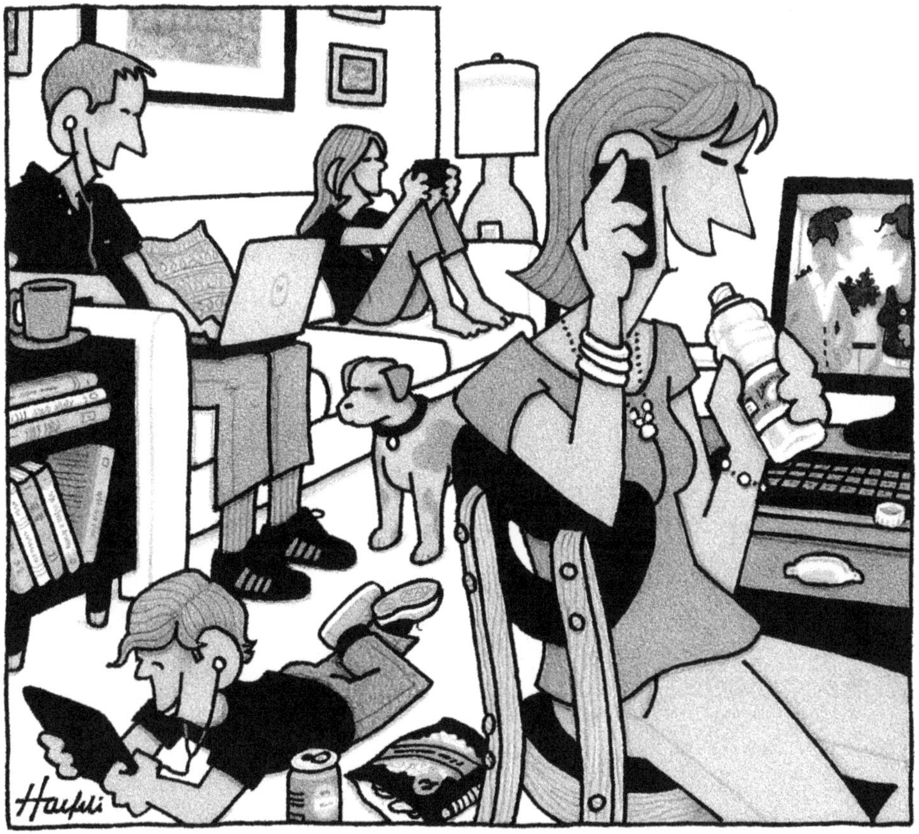
Haefeli

"We're all together watching television,
but we're not all watching television together."

"Kids! No watching Bobby Flay before Mommy cooks dinner!"

"We're hoping that someday Rosalie will be
a major player in the creative economy."

"One day you'll thank me for embarrassing
you in front of the entire Internet."

"O.K., now—on three, I'm going to toss a second job in there!"

"You're right—this is way better than a standing desk."

"Here's the deal: we call the shots when you're young, you call the shots when we're old, and everything in between is a non-stop battle for control."

"I dreamed I was being chased by a giant standardized test."

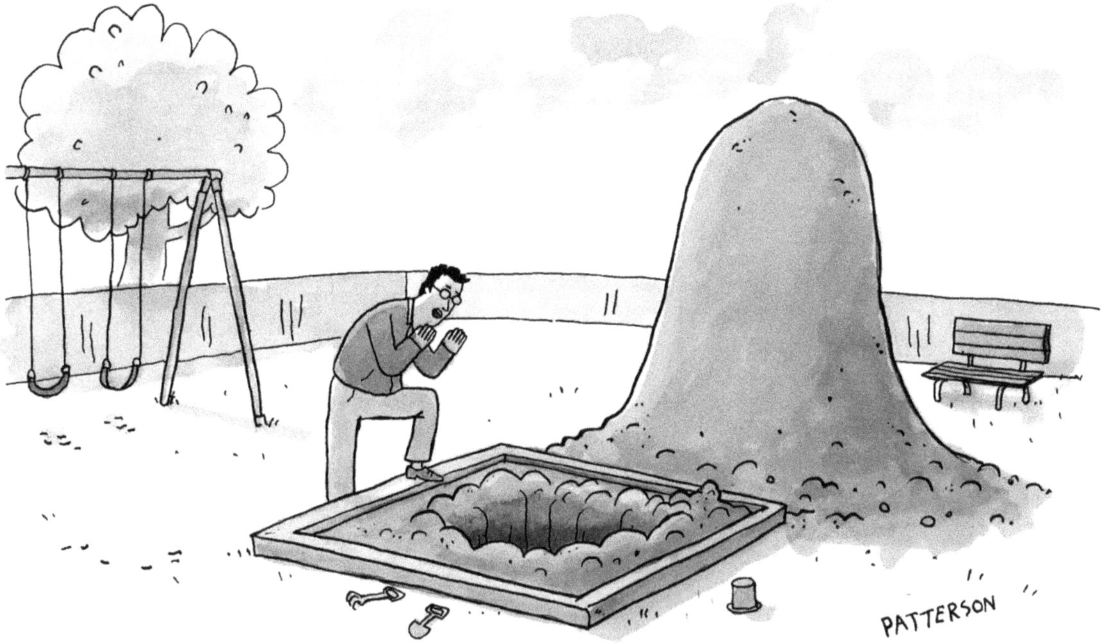
PATTERSON

"O.K., Peter, time to go."

"You were always my favorite to manipulate."

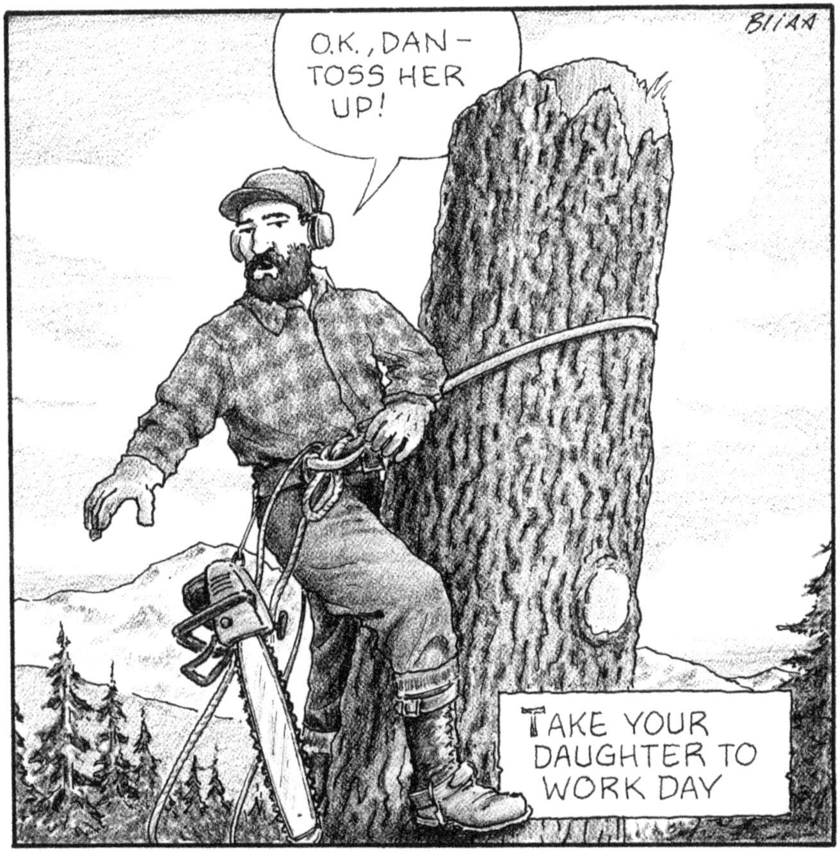
O.K., DAN-
TOSS HER
UP!
TAKE YOUR
DAUGHTER TO
WORK DAY

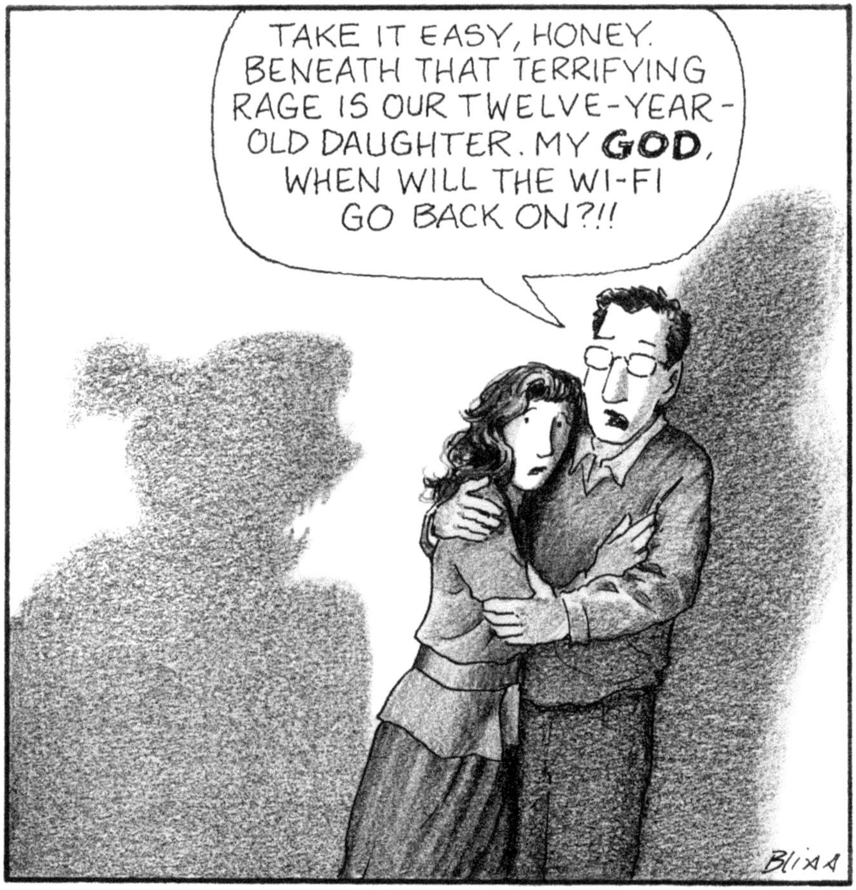
TAKE IT EASY, HONEY. BENEATH THAT TERRIFYING RAGE IS OUR TWELVE-YEAR-OLD DAUGHTER. MY **GOD**, WHEN WILL THE WI-FI GO BACK ON?!!
BLISS

"This tantrum has been powerful, honest and riveting, and I think we should just give him what he wants."

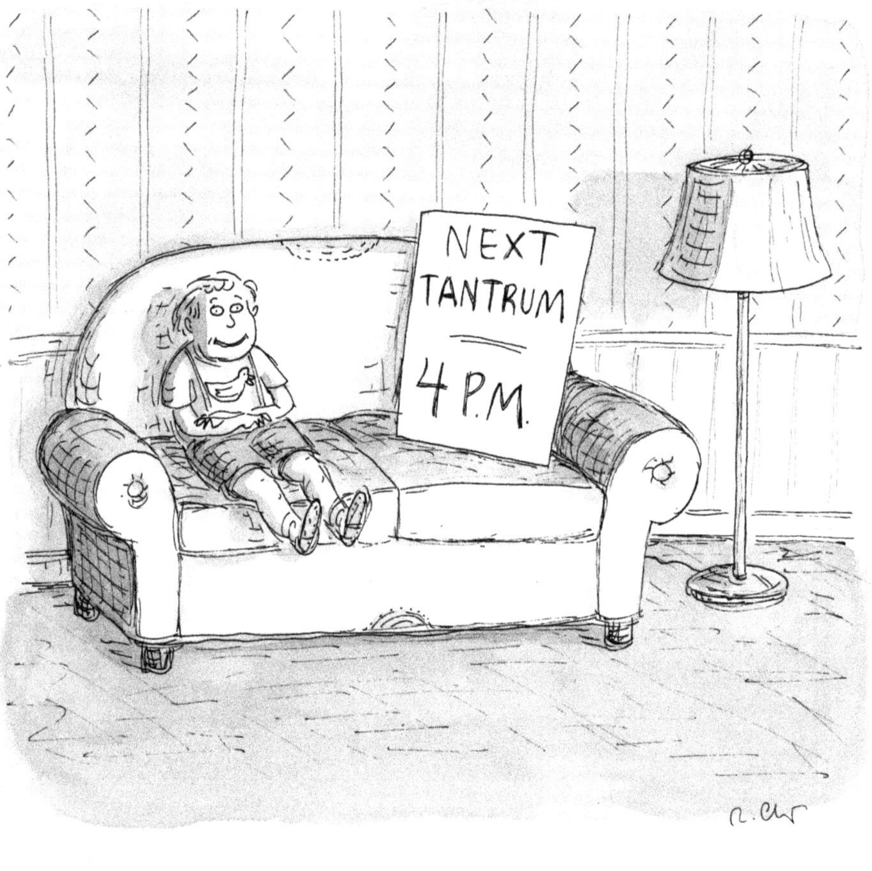
NEXT
TANTRUM
4 P.M.

"*Now that I have it all, I'd like to scale it back a bit.*"

"*Why are people with kids always telling everyone else to have kids?*"

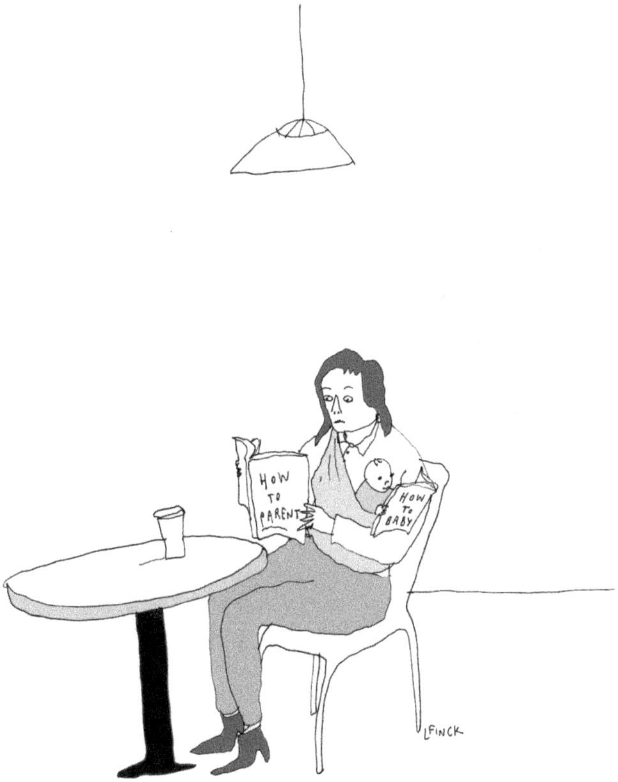
HOW
TO
PARENT
HOW
TO
BABY
LFINCK

"These are payments for babysitters, but it's more exciting to pretend I'm a drug dealer."

"*I love you too, Daddy, but it just kills me that you're a man.*"

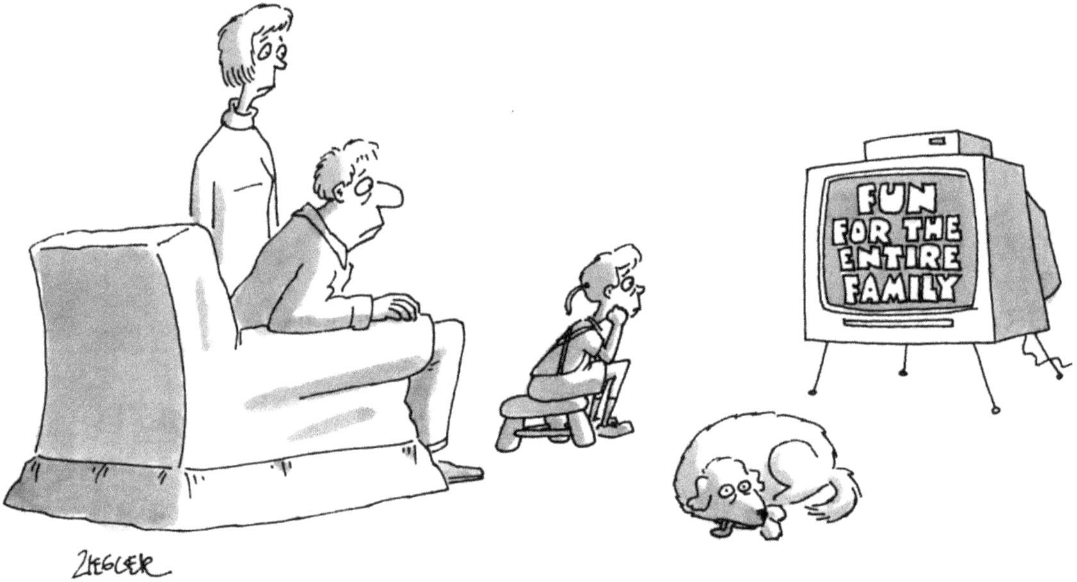
FUN
FOR THE
ENTIRE
FAMILY
ZIEGLER

"Dear, I hope you don't think I'm too old-fashioned, but do you think you could call me 'Grandmother' or 'Grandma' instead of 'Butt-Head'?"

THINGS *NOT* TO TELL YOUR KID

Sometimes we drink milk from cows and sometimes we drink milk from horses like the ones in Central Park.

There's a big stopper at the bottom of the ocean, and every once in a while it gets accidentally pulled out.

Isn't this FUN?

"The Wizard of Oz" is a true story.

Anything electrical can suddenly BLOW UP for no reason whatsoever.

TICK
TICK
TICK
TICK

r. Chast

"I've called the family together to announce that, because of inflation,
I'm going to have to let two of you go."

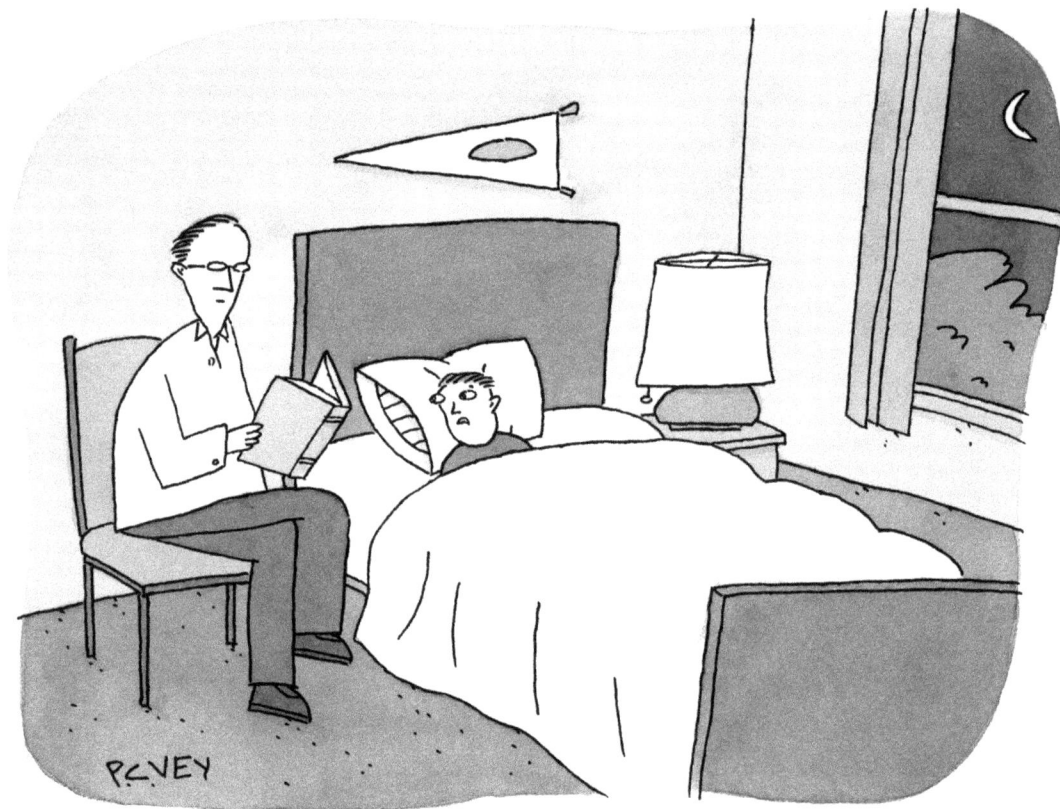

"Shouldn't you be reading that to me out loud or something?"

"Your mother and I are feeling overwhelmed, so you'll have to bring yourselves up."

"Daddy's way of helping you with your homework is not to help you."

"He's just doing that to get attention."

"Instead of 'It sucks' you should say, 'It doesn't speak to me.'"

TANTRUM SCENE · DO NOT CROSS

KOREN

"Before we begin this family meeting, how about we go around
and say our names and a little something about ourselves."

CHILD FROM ANOTHER PLANET

"*After I introduce you to solids, I'm going to need your help with some computer stuff.*"

"We can't leave her with my parents! Do you want her to turn out
like me?"

"Look, just finish college, get your MBA, have a career, and then
if you want to try acting, you'll have my blessing."

UNFORTUNATELY, AT THIS AGE I EXPRESS GLEE AND STARK RAVING TERROR IN THE EXACT SAME WAY.

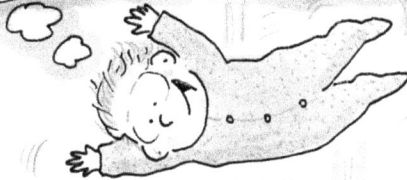

"My parents are members of a tiny cult that worships me."

"Marcy, you hurt Tommy's self esteem when you say there's a monster under your bed."

"When the evil witch pushes the children into the oven,
.... that's just a metaphor for putting them in the microwave."

"This time can the tooth fairy
please just Venmo me?"

"I'm warning you—peas and carrots are gateway vegetables."

"Ten more minutes of media manipulation, then it's off to bed."

"Marcy's making a live Mother's Day Webcast!"

"Jimmy has helicopter parents."

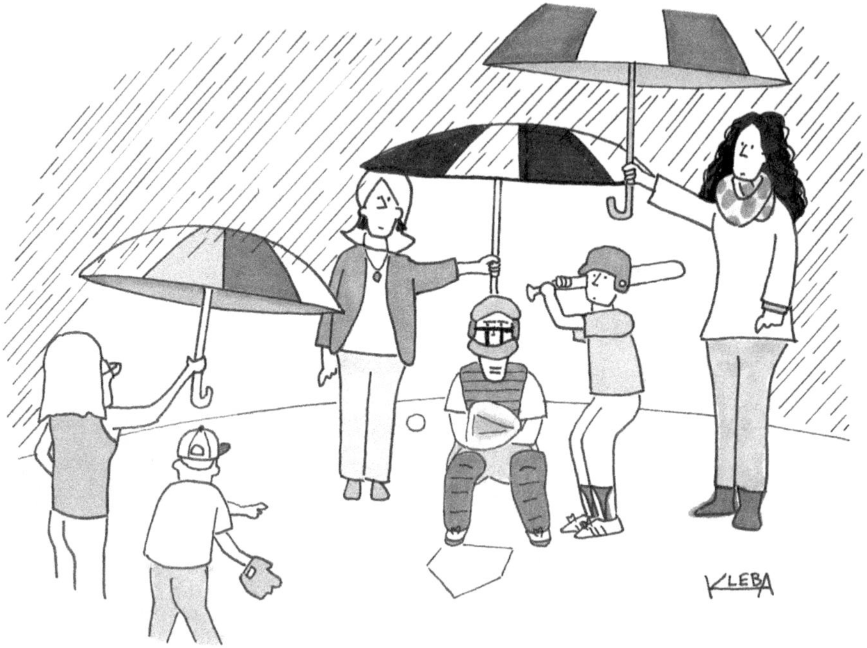
KLEBA

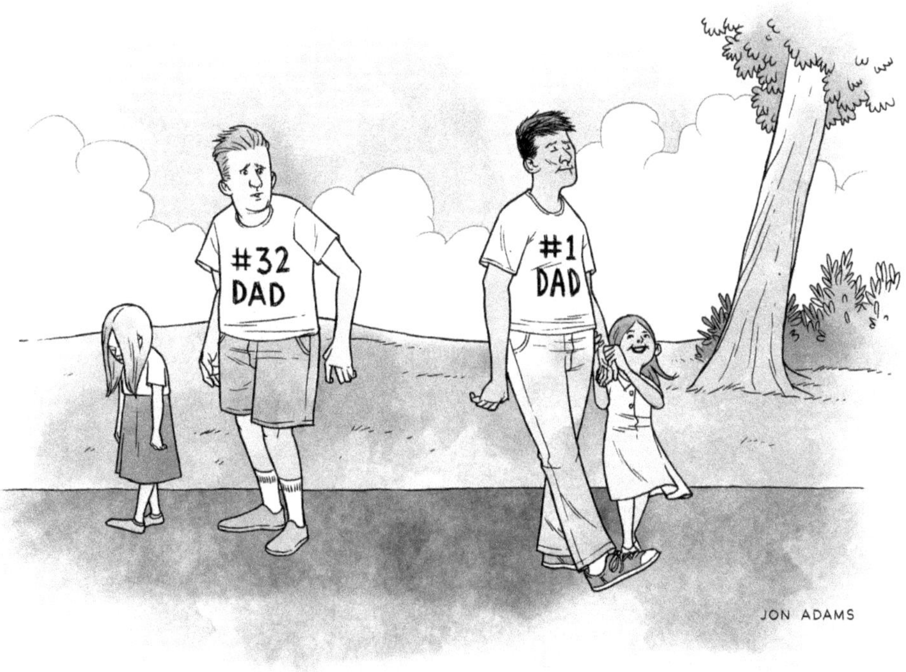
#32
DAD
#1
DAD
JON ADAMS

"Before you know it they've got legs and
they're swimming all over the place."

"I worry that monkey bars aren't safe."

WILL SANTINO

"Hey, I love my daughters too but you gotta set boundaries."

"She's changed so much since the sonogram."

"We're trying to limit our kids' screen time to 23 hours a day."

"I live underneath your kid's bed and he's beginning to scare me."

"By our estimates, it's going to take two villages to raise Joey."

"Oh, let it go, Steve. It's just a phase."

"Before texting we had to write letters by hand, and before emojis we honestly just bottled up our emotions."

"I'm pretty sure having your child ride rear-facing
until they're four only applies to car seats."

P. BYRNES.

"Did you know that when my mom played soccer,
only the winner got a trophy?"

"The s-p-e-l-l-i-n-g thing doesn't w-o-r-k anymore, mom."

"Why don't you go turn on your toys
and watch them play."

P. BYRNES.

"Jenny, your play date's here!"

"No! Instagram was enough!
I don't want to know about Tik Tok!"

Index of Artists

www.ingramcontent.com/pod-product-compliance
Lightning Source LLC
Chambersburg PA
CBHW060759150426
42813CB00058B/2737